Summer
Drinks

Summer Drinks

Over 100 refreshing recipes to enjoy in the sunshine

RYLAND PETERS & SMALL
LONDON • NEW YORK

Senior Designer Toni Kay
Production Manager Gordana
  Simakovic
Art Director Leslie Harrington
Editorial Director Julia Charles
Publisher Cindy Richards
Indexer Hilary Bird

First published in 2021
by Ryland Peters & Small,
20–21 Jockey's Fields,
London WC1R 4BW
and
341 E 116th St,
New York NY 10029

www.rylandpeters.com

10 9 8 7 6 5 4 3 2 1

Recipe collection compiled by
Julia Charles. Recipes © copyright
Valerie Aikman-Smith, Julia Charles,
Jesses Estes, Ursula Ferrigno, Ben
Fordham & Felipe Fuentes Cruz,
Laura Gladwin, Victoria Glass, Nicola
Graimes, Beshlie Grimes, Hannah
Miles, Louise Pickford, James Porter,
Ben Reed and David T. Smith 2021.
Design and photographs © Ryland
Peters & Small 2021. See page 144
for full text and picture credits.

ISBN: 978-1-78879-358-2

A CIP record for this book is
available from the British Library.

US Library of Congress cataloging-
in-publication data has been
applied for.

Printed and bound in China.

Notes

• Both metric and imperial oz./
US cups are included. Work with
one set of measurements and do
not alternate between the two within
a recipe. All spoon measurements
given are level:
1 tsp (teaspoon) = 5 ml
1 tbsp (tablespoon) = 15 ml

• Uncooked or partially cooked eggs
should not be served to the elderly
or frail, young children, pregnant
women or those with compromised
immune systems.

• When a recipe calls for citrus zest
or peel, buy unwaxed fruit and wash
well before using. If you can only find
treated fruit, scrub well in warm
soapy water before using.

• To sterilize screw-top jars and
bottles to store syrups and cordials,
preheat the oven to 160°C/150°C
fan/325°F/Gas 3. Wash the jars and/
or bottles and their lids in hot soapy
water then rinse but don't dry them.
Remove any rubber seals, put the jars
onto a baking sheet and into the oven
for 10 minutes. Soak the lids in boiling
water for a few minutes.

Contents

Introduction

Come the summer months the rising temperatures mean the pace of life slows right down. The long, lazy days might find us reading in a shady spot in the garden, lounging by an azure-blue swimming pool, enjoying a sundowner on a porch swing or dining al fresco under a star-filled sky. Refreshing drinks, served over ice or sipped from a freezer-frosted glass, offer not just refreshment but the thrill of lip-tingling pleasure. Whether enjoyed on the lawn or poolside, on a balcony or rooftop terrace, your drinks should be full of the vibrant flavours and colours of summer.

The warmest season can bring invitations to a host of events from cook-outs and pool parties, to elegant garden parties and weddings. Come your turn to host any of these gatherings you may find yourself looking for inspiration beyond the hastily assembled choices of warm white wine, a bucket of beers and overly sugary soft drinks. Here, in this collection of delightfully sunshine-filled drinks, you'll find recipes to cater for every summer occasion. Choose from sparkling aperitifs, tangy citrus-based cocktails, refreshingly fizzy spritzes and highballs, crowd-pleasing pitchers, deliciously fruity mocktails and juices, as well as fun slushies and floats that offer a nostalgic reminder of carefree childhood summers. In addition, the flavoured syrups on pages 8–9 used alone are perfect for rustling up easy drinks, just pour them over ice and top them up with soda water, tonic or sparkling wine for effortless refreshment throughout the summer.

The recipe methods themselves are easy to follow and require no specialist equipment. That said, any home bartender can always use a cocktail shaker and a measuring jigger. Wine glasses are useful all-rounders and Champagne flutes are ideal for sparkling aperitifs but you may also want a few pieces of glassware especially designed for iconic cocktails, such as Margarita coupes and hurricane glasses. Also useful are balloon (copa) glasses for serving spritzes and gin and tonics. You might also consider acrylic or bamboo drinking cups and pitchers if you are worried about breakages – there are plenty of attractive styles to choose from in a fiesta of colours. Have fun with garnishing your drinks too. Make them visually appealing with citrus slices, fresh berries, edible flowers and pineapple leaves, and, if the occasion calls for it, why not accessorize your creations with paper straws and novelty stirrers? And lastly, ice, you'll need plenty of ice! Stock up on ice cube trays, make ice in batches and consider a delivery of ready-made cubes or crushed ice if you need large quantities.

We hope you enjoy this sunshine recipe collection and discover delicious new ways to keep your cool throughout the long, hot summer ahead.

Syrup recipes

Sugar syrup

225 g/1 cup white sugar
250 ml/1 cup water

Add the sugar and water to a small saucepan. Bring to the boil and let simmer until clear and slightly thickened. Take off the heat and allow to cool. Store in a sterilized screwtop jar (see page 4) for up to 4 weeks.

Strawberry syrup

225 g/1 cup white sugar
250 ml/1 cup water
125 g/4½ oz. fresh strawberries, chopped

Add the sugar and water to a small saucepan. Bring to the boil and let simmer until clear and slightly thickened. Take off the heat and stir in the strawberries. Leave to cool, strain and discard the strawberries. Transfer to a sterilized screwtop jar (see page 4) and store in the fridge for up to 2 weeks.

Raspberry syrup

200 g/1½ cups fresh raspberries
500 g/2½ cups white sugar
500 ml/2 cups boiling water

Muddle the fresh raspberries in the base of a heatproof jug/pitcher. Add the sugar and boiling water and stir until the sugar has dissolved. Allow to cool and then pass the syrup through a strainer/sieve and discard the seeds. Transfer to a sterilized screwtop jar (see page 4) and store in the fridge for up to 2 weeks.

Watermelon & rosé syrup

125 ml/½ cup sweet, fruity rosé wine
(a Californian Zinfandel works well)

125 ml/½ cup fresh watermelon juice
(see page 84)

250 g/1¼ cups white sugar

Combine the wine, watermelon juice and sugar in a saucepan and set over a medium heat. Bring to the boil, stirring, until the sugar dissolves. Turn off the heat and leave to cool. Strain and discard any pulp or seeds. Transfer to a sterilized screwtop jar (see page 4) and store in the fridge for up to 2 weeks.

Pineapple syrup

500 g/2½ cups white sugar

300 ml/1¼ cups water

1 small pineapple, peeled, cored and chopped

Add the sugar and water to a small saucepan. Bring to the boil and let simmer until clear and slightly thickened. Take off the heat and add the pineapple. Leave to cool, and then to infuse for a few hours and ideally overnight. Strain and discard the pineapple. Transfer to a sterilized screwtop jar (see page 4) and store in the fridge for up to 2 weeks.

Goji berry syrup

500 ml/2 cups water

250 g/2¼ cups dried goji berries

500 g/2½ cups white sugar

Add the water and goji berries to a saucepan and bring to the boil. Remove from the heat and leave to infuse for a few minutes. Strain out the berries and discard them. Add the sugar and stir until dissolved. Allow to cool. Transfer to a sterilized screwtop jar (see page 4) and store in the fridge for up to 3 weeks.

Hibiscus syrup

500 g/2½ cups white sugar

500 ml/2 cups water

75 g/1 cup dried hibiscus flowers

Add the ingredients to a saucepan and bring to the boil. Remove from the heat and stir. Allow to cool, strain and discard the flowers. Transfer to a sterilized screwtop jar (see page 4) and store in the fridge for up to 3 weeks.

Aperitifs & Cocktails

Cocomango

15 ml/½ oz. coconut white rum, such as Malibu

15 ml/½ oz. gin

30 ml/1 oz. mango juice

10 ml/⅓ oz. freshly squeezed lime juice

a dash of Angostura bitters (optional)

chilled Asti Spumante or other semi-sweet sparkling wine, to top up

a dried mango strip, to garnish

SERVES 1

This delicious taste of the tropics is a lighter and more quaffable alternative to coconut-based, tiki-style drinks so enjoy as a summer aperitif.

Pour the first 5 ingredients into a cocktail shaker with a handful of ice cubes and shake well. Strain into a Champagne flute and top up with Asti Spumante.

Garnish with a strip of dried mango and serve at once.

Mango daiquiri

6 fresh mangoes, or equivalent amount of frozen mango flesh

350 ml/1½ cups light rum

sugar syrup, to taste (see page 8)

SERVES 4

This frozen daiquiri is Beachside Baja California in a glass – use either fresh or frozen mango.

Put 4 cocktail glasses in the freezer to chill.

If using fresh mangoes, peel and stone/pit the mangoes, then slice. Put the flesh into a blender with an equal volume of ice and whizz until you have a smooth purée. Add the rum, and sugar syrup to taste, then pulse again. Pour at once into the chilled glasses and serve.

If using frozen mango, put it straight into the blender with half the volume of ice. Whizz until you have a smooth purée. Add the rum, and sugar syrup to taste, pulse again. Pour at once into the chilled glasses and serve at once.

Florida breeze

35 ml/1¼ oz. pink grapefruit juice

15 ml/½ oz. sweet red vermouth

a dash of sugar syrup
  (see page 8)

a dash of Angostura bitters

chilled Cava or other dry
  sparkling wine, to top up

a grapefruit zest, to garnish
  (optional)

SERVES 1

The tartness of pink grapefruit awakens the appetite perfectly here. What summer lunch with friends wouldn't benefit from a little Florida sparkle?

Pour the first 4 ingredients into a cocktail shaker with a handful of ice cubes and shake well. Strain into a chilled Champagne flute, top up with Cava and serve at once.

St Clement's fizz

10 ml/⅓ oz. Cointreau

10 ml/⅓ oz. limoncello

10 ml/⅓ oz. Aperol

a dash of orange bitters (optional)

chilled Prosecco or other
  dry sparkling wine, to top

lemon and orange zests, to garnish

SERVES 1

This zesty creation really does sing of oranges and lemons, and makes a fabulous aperitif that will happily lend its dose of citrus sunshine to any occasion.

Pour the first 4 ingredients into a cocktail shaker with a handful of ice cubes and stir well. Strain into a chilled Champagne flute and top up with Prosecco. Garnish with orange and lemon zests and serve at once.

Peach julep

5 fresh mint leaves

20 ml/⅔ oz. bourbon

30 ml/1 oz. peach juice

5 ml/1 tsp peach schnapps

chilled Champagne or other
  dry sparkling wine, to top up

a peach slice, to garnish

SERVES 1

In the 19th century, mint juleps were sometimes made with peach brandy, and this refreshingly minty sparkler takes its inspiration from them. Perfect for hot summer nights.

Muddle the mint leaves with the bourbon in a cocktail shaker. Add the peach juice and peach schnapps with a handful of ice cubes and shake well.

Strain into a chilled Champagne coupe, garnish with a peach slice and serve at once.

Prosecco passion

30 ml/1 oz. vanilla vodka

5 ml/1 tsp sugar syrup
  (see page 8)

1 passion fruit

chilled Prosecco, to top up

a vanilla pod/bean, to garnish
  (optional)

SERVES 1

Here's a twist on that absolute cocktail classic, the Porn Star. If you love the indulgence and sweetness of passion fruit, then this is the summer sparkler for you! (See photo on page 10.)

Put the vodka and sugar syrup in a cocktail shaker. Halve the passion fruit, scoop out all the pulp and seeds and drop them into the shaker. Add a handful of ice cubes and shake.

Strain into a chilled Martini glass, top up with Prosecco, garnish with a vanilla pod/bean (if using) and serve at once.

Seventh heaven

5 fresh mint leaves

5 ml/1 tsp sugar syrup
  (see page 8)

1 tsp freshly squeezed lemon juice

30 ml/1 oz. pineapple juice

30 ml/1 oz. sweet red vermouth

chilled Prosecco or other
  dry sparkling wine, to top up

a small pineapple wedge, to
  garnish (optional)

SERVES 1

Sweet vermouth and fresh mint provide the ideal backdrop for the tropical flavours in this chic cocktail that will keep your guests guessing.

Muddle the mint leaves, sugar syrup and lemon juice in a cocktail shaker. Add the pineapple juice and vermouth with a handful of ice cubes and shake well.

Strain into a chilled Champagne flute and top up with Prosecco. Garnish with a long, thin wedge of pineapple, if you like, and serve at once.

Pineapple margarita

½ ripe fresh pineapple, chilled

freshly squeezed juice of 2 limes

120 ml/4 oz. Cointreau or
  triple sec

235 ml/1 cup blanco tequila

agave syrup, to taste (optional)

pineapple wedges, to decorate

SERVES 4

A frothy and fruity tasting version of a Margarita, this drink is also known as Pineapple Fluff. Try to use a super-sweet pineapple for the best result.

Put 4 cocktail glasses in the freezer to chill.

Cut the half pineapple into 4 wedges lengthways. Run the knife along the peel of each wedge to remove, then cut the pineapple into chunks.

Put the pineapple, lime juice, Cointreau or triple sec and tequila in a blender with a few ice cubes and whizz up to a smooth, frothy mix. Add a little agave syrup if it needs some sweetening. Pour into chilled glasses, garnish each drink with a pineapple wedge and serve at once.

Sbagliato

30 ml/1 oz. red Italian vermouth

30 ml/1 oz. Campari

75 ml/2½ oz. chilled Prosecco

SERVES 1

Sbagliato means 'mistaken' in Italian and in this, apparently accidental, but rather delicious variation of a classic Negroni cocktail, the gin is replaced with sparkling Prosecco.

Fill an old-fashioned glass with ice cubes and add the vermouth and Campari. Stir well. Add the Prosecco and stir very gently to preserve the fizz. Serve at once.

Tiziano

10 seedless red grapes

75 ml/2½ oz. Dubonnet

chilled Prosecco, to top up

a strip of orange zest, to garnish

SERVES 1

This gorgeous concoction would be just perfect to kick off an intimate meal à deux. Dubonnet's Rouge Aperitif wine has been a staple on the cocktail landscape since 1846, and rightly so!

Put 9 of the grapes into a cocktail shaker and muddle them to crush and extract the juice. Add a handful of ice cubes and the Dubonnet and shake vigorously. Strain into an old-fashioned glass, add some ice cubes and top up with Prosecco. Squeeze the orange zest lengthways to spritz the essential oils in the skin over the drink. Garnish with the zest and the remaining grape and serve at once.

Watermelon martini

160 g/1 cup cubed ripe
watermelon

60 ml/2 oz. vodka

sugar syrup, to taste (see page 8)

a small watermelon slice, to
garnish

SERVES 1

Who could forget the immortal line of Baby
in Dirty Dancing: 'I carried a watermelon'? Why
not keep out of the heat and watch a feel-good
summer movie whilst sipping this deliciously
refreshing cocktail?

Muddle the watermelon flesh in a cocktail shaker, add
the vodka and a handful of ice cubes and shake sharply.
Taste and add sugar syrup if you'd like it sweeter. Strain
into a Martini glass, garnish with a slice of watermelon
and serve at once.

Cucumber martini

12-cm/5-in. piece of cucumber,
peeled and roughly chopped

2 tbsp sugar syrup (see page 8)

6 fresh mint leaves

1 tbsp freshly squeezed
lemon juice

60 ml/2 oz. vodka

SERVES 2

This light and fresh-tasting twist on a classic
Martini makes the perfect summer cooler.

Put the cucumber, sugar syrup, mint leaves and lemon
juice in a blender and process until smooth.

Add a handful of ice cubes to a cocktail shaker and
pour in the cucumber mix, along with the vodka. Shake
vigorously, strain into Martini glasses and serve at once.

Hibiscus martini

~~~~~~~~~~~~~~~~~

30 ml/1 oz. vodka

5 ml/1 tsp freshly squeezed lime juice

a dash of framboise liqueur

60 ml/2 oz. hibiscus syrup (see page 9)

a food-safe hibiscus flower, to garnish (optional)

SERVES 1

The hibiscus flower is big, bold, bright and beautiful. Not only does it make a delicious cocktail, it also makes a gorgeous summer hair accessory. Simply tuck one behind your ear and you're good to go!

Add all the ingredients to a cocktail shaker with a handful of ice cubes. Shake and strain into a Martini glass. Garnish with a hibiscus flower (if using) and serve at once.

Hibiscus G & T

~~~~~~~~~~~~~~~~~

2 tbsp hibiscus syrup (see page 9)

60 ml/2 oz. gin

about 200 ml/7 oz. chilled Indian tonic water

food-safe hibiscus flowers, to garnish (optional)

SERVES 2

A Hawaiian take on an English classic.

Half fill 2 highball glasses or tumblers with ice cubes. Put 1 tbsp of hibiscus syrup into each glass. Add 30 ml/1 oz. of gin to each, divide the tonic between the glasses and stir well. Garnish each glass with a hibiscus flower (if using) and serve at once.

Tommy's margarita

a lime wedge

sea salt flakes, to rim the glass

50 ml/1²⁄₃ oz. blanco tequila

30 ml/1 oz. freshly squeezed
lime juice

30 ml/1 oz. mixed agave syrup
(a 75:25 mix of agave syrup and
water, to make pouring easier)

SERVES 1

This twist on the classic Margarita removes the
orange liqueur element and adds agave syrup.

Rim a Margarita glass with the salt by first running the lime
wedge around the rim and then placing the glass upside
down on a saucer of the salt, leaving a light covering around
the edge of the glass. Put all the ingredients in a cocktail
shaker and add a handful of ice cubes. Shake hard then
strain into the prepared glass. To garnish, cut a small nick
in the lime wedge and slide it onto the rim of the glass.
Serve at once.

Spicy green margarita

a lime wedge

sea salt flakes, to rim the glass

8 fresh mint leaves, plus a small
sprig to garnish

10 coriander/cilantro leaves

a tiny piece of habanero chilli/chile

15 ml/½ oz. mixed agave syrup
(a 75:25 mix of agave syrup and
water, to make pouring easier)

35 ml/1¼ oz. blanco tequila

25 ml/³⁄₄ oz. fresh pineapple juice

25 ml/³⁄₄ oz. freshly squeezed
lime juice

SERVES 1

A tropical, herby, citrusy, spicy Margarita that slips
down all too easily but be warned, it's hot, hot, hot!

Rim a Margarita glass with the salt by first running the
lime wedge around the rim and then placing the glass
upside down on a saucer of the salt, leaving a light
covering around the edge of the glass. Muddle together
the mint, coriander/cilantro, chilli/chile and the mixed
agave syrup in a cocktail shaker. Combine with all the
remaining ingredients and shake hard with a handful of
ice cubes. Strain into the glass, garnish with a mint sprig
and serve at once.

Variation: This also makes a great non-alcoholic drink
(agua fresca). Simply replace the tequila with apple juice
and then top up with sparkling water in a highball glass.

Pisco sour

120 ml/4 oz. Pisco

60 ml/2 oz. freshly squeezed
lime juice

2 egg whites

45 ml/1½ oz. sugar syrup
(see page 8)

a dash of Angostura bitters

lime wheels, to garnish

SERVES 2

The Pisco Sour originates in Lima and it could be
considered Peru's national drink. Pisco – a spirit
distilled from grapes – has a bright, lively flavour.
Mixed with lime, it makes a really nice cocktail
to be sipped slowly as the sun goes down.

Fill a cocktail shaker with ice cubes and pour in the
Pisco, lime juice, egg whites and sugar syrup. Shake
vigorously and strain into 2 rocks glasses or tumblers.

Top each drink with a dash of Angostura bitters, garnish
with lime wheels and serve at once.

Sour Italian

30 ml/1 oz. Campari

15 ml/½ oz. Strega

15 ml/½ oz. Galliano

25 ml/¾ oz. freshly squeezed
lemon juice

15 ml/½ oz. cranberry juice

15 ml/½ oz. sugar syrup
(see page 8)

a dash of egg white

2 dashes of Angostura bitters

SERVES 2

A cocktail made from all-Italian ingredients, the
Sour Italian makes a lovely summer aperitif.

Put all of the ingredients into a cocktail shaker and
add a handful of ice cubes. Shake vigorously, strain
into 2 Champagne flutes or small wine glasses and
serve at once.

Pomegranate margarita

a lime wedge and equal parts mixed sugar and sea salt flakes, to rim the glass

50 ml/1²/₃ oz. blanco tequila

20 ml/²/₃ oz. freshly squeezed lime juice

20 ml/²/₃ oz. triple sec

25 ml/³/₄ oz. pomegranate juice

food-safe rose petals, to garnish (optional)

SERVES 1

The pomegranate gives this drink a beautiful pink hue and provides a crisp, dry acidity. Perfect to enjoy poolside or on the beach.

Rub a lime wedge around the rim of a coupe glass, then dip the outer edge of the rim into the mixed sugar and salt. Set aside.

Shake all the ingredients in a cocktail shaker with a handful of ice cubes and strain into the prepared glass. Garnish with a few rose petals (if using) and serve at once.

Ancho margarita

a lime wedge and smoked sea salt flakes, to rim the glass

50 ml/1²/₃ oz. blanco tequila

25 ml/³/₄ oz. freshly squeezed lime juice

25 ml/³/₄ oz. Ancho Reyes Chile Liqueur, or similar

a dehydrated lime wheel, to garnish

SERVES 1

A winning combination of tequila, lime, ancho chilli/chile and salt.

Rub the rim of a chilled coupe glass with a lime wedge. Roll the outer edge of the glass rim in the smoked sea salt flakes and set aside.

Add all the ingredients to a cocktail shaker with a handful of ice cubes and shake hard. Fine strain into the prepared glass. Garnish with a dehydrated lime wheel and serve at once.

Lion's tail

45 ml/1½ oz. Wild Turkey 80 Proof Bourbon, or similar

25 ml/¾ oz. freshly squeezed lime juice

15 ml/½ oz. sugar syrup (see page 8)

10 ml/2 tsp yellow Chartreuse

5 dashes of pimento dram (allspice liqueur)

a lime zest, to garnish

SERVES 1

This largely forgotten classic cocktail was first published in the Café Royal Cocktail Book in 1937. Here some Yellow Chartreuse has been added to the basic recipe as the herbaceous and saffron notes interplay beautifully with the bourbon and pimento dram (allspice liqueur).

Combine all the ingredients in a cocktail shaker with a handful of ice cubes and shake hard. Strain into a chilled coupe glass, garnish with a lime zest and serve at once.

Honi honi

50 ml/1⅔ oz. Buffalo Trace Bourbon, or similar

25 ml/¾ oz. freshly squeezed lime juice

15 ml/½ oz. Cointreau

15 ml/½ oz. orgeat (almond syrup)

a fresh pineapple spear, fresh mint sprig, orange slice, maraschino cherry and a dusting of icing/ confectioners' sugar, to garnish

SERVES 1

Honi honi means 'kiss kiss' in Tahitian. This is essentially a Mai Tai cocktail made with bourbon instead of rum. It's superbly refreshing and dangerously easy to drink.

Combine all the ingredients in a cocktail shaker with a handful of ice cubes and shake. Strain into a Tiki mug or rocks glass over crushed ice. Cap with more crushed ice and garnish with a pineapple spear, mint sprig, orange slice and cherry. Dust with icing/ confectioners' sugar and serve at once.

Spritzes
& Coolers

Spanish fruit cup

100 ml/3⅓ oz. chilled fruity rosé wine (a Spanish Garnacha works well)

50 ml/1¾ oz. freshly squeezed orange juice, strained

10 ml/¼ oz. Spanish brandy

10 ml/¼ oz. Cointreau

200 ml/¾–1 cup Fever-Tree Mediterranean tonic water, (or any tonic water of your choice)

orange and lemon wheels, green apple slices and a strawberry slice, to garnish

SERVES 1

Here is a fresh and lighter take on a classic red-wine sangria, made with a fruity rosé wine.

Pour all of the ingredients, adding the tonic last, into a large balloon/copa glass (or large wine glass) half-filled with ice cubes and stir gently. Add the fruit slices and garnish the rim of the glass with a strawberry slice. Serve at once.

Variation: This also makes a wonderful pitcher drink, so simply use a 750-ml/25-oz. bottle of rosé wine and multiply the other ingredients by 7 to serve 6–8.

The perfect spritz

35 ml/1¼ oz. Aperol

75 ml/2½ oz. chilled Prosecco

soda water, to top up

an orange slice, to garnish

MAKES 1

Make your next Aperol spritz this way rather than follow the directions on the bottle, as the Italians knew what they were doing when they came up with this method! (See photo on page 34.)

Half-fill a large balloon/copa glass (or large wine glass) with ice cubes. Pour in the Aperol and half the Prosecco and stir gently. Add the rest of the Prosecco and a splash of soda, garnish with an orange slice and serve at once.

Rosé spritz

50 ml/1²⁄₃ oz. Aperol

25 ml/¾ oz. passion fruit juice
(such as Rubicon)

1 tsp freshly squeezed lime juice

75 ml/2½ oz. chilled rosé Prosecco

lime wedges, to serve

SERVES 1

This recipe peps up the popular Aperol spritz with the addition of sparkling rosé Prosecco, fragrant passion fruit juice and just a hint of zesty lime juice. The perfect refreshment on a hot summer's day.

Half-fill a large balloon/copa glass (or large wine glass) with ice cubes. Pour in the Aperol, passion fruit juice and lime juice. Stir and top up with the rosé Prosecco. Garnish with a couple of wedges of lime and serve at once.

Strawberry spritz

15 ml/½ oz. strawberry syrup
(see page 8)

50 ml/1²⁄₃ oz. Aperol

75 ml/2½ oz. chilled fruity rosé
wine (a Chilean Cabernet-based
blend works well)

15 ml/½ oz. freshly squeezed
lemon juice

about 200 ml/¾–1 cup soda water

strawberry and lemon slices,
to garnish

SERVES 1

A gentler version of The Perfect Spritz (see page 37) that is deliciously light, fresh and fruity with an enticing strawberry scent.

Pour the strawberry syrup into a highball glass. Add the Aperol, rosé and lemon juice and stir. Add plenty of ice cubes and top with up with soda water to taste, but no more than 200 ml/¾–1 cup. Garnish with strawberry and lemon slices and serve at once.

Paloma

a lime wedge and sea salt flakes, to rim the glass

50 ml/1²⁄₃ oz. blanco tequila

2 tsp freshly squeezed lime juice

grapefruit soda (such as Squirt, Ting or Three Cents), to top up

a pink grapefruit slice, to garnish

SERVES 1

While the Margarita is the most well-known tequila cocktail outside of Mexico, the Paloma is likely the most popular tequila-based mixed drink in Mexico and it is now becoming increasingly popular in bars worldwide.

Prepare a highball glass by rubbing the rim with a lime wedge, then dip the rim of the glass into the sea salt flakes. Combine all the ingredients in the prepared glass over plenty of ice cubes. Stir well to mix and chill the drink. Garnish with a pink grapefruit slice and serve at once.

Jalisco siesta

30 ml/1 oz. freshly squeezed lemon juice

15 ml/¹⁄₂ oz. agave syrup

5 fresh mint leaves, plus an extra sprig to garnish

50 ml/1²⁄₃ oz. reposado (aged) tequila

50 ml/1²⁄₃ oz. ginger beer

SERVES 1

This crisp, refreshing drink is a variation of the mojito using tequila instead of rum and with the spicy addition of ginger beer.

Add the lemon juice, agave syrup and mint leaves to a highball glass and muddle gently. Fill the glass with crushed ice and add the tequila and ginger beer. Stir gently, garnish with a mint sprig and serve at once.

Airmail

35 ml/1¼ oz. dark rum

15 ml/½ oz. freshly squeezed lime juice

10 ml/⅓ oz. honey mixed with 1 tsp boiling water

chilled Prosecco, or other dry sparkling white wine, to top up

a lime slice, to garnish

SERVES 1

This transporting combination of sparkling white wine, fresh lime juice and dark rum is as refreshing as it is sophisticated.

Put the rum, lime juice and honey mixture in an old-fashioned glass, add a handful of ice cubes and stir. Top up with Prosecco, garnish with a lime slice and serve at once.

Sparkling mojito

10 fresh mint leaves, plus extra to garnish

1 tsp white sugar

½ lime, cut into wedges

35 ml/1¼ oz. white rum

chilled Prosecco or other dry sparkling white wine, to top up

SERVES 1

Everything you love about a mojito, with a dash of Prosecco in the mix instead of soda water to add some sparkle to the proceedings.

Put the mint leaves, sugar and lime wedges in a highball glass and muddle well. Add the rum, stir and fill the glass with crushed ice. Top up with Prosecco and stir very gently. Garnish with lightly crushed mint leaves and serve at once.

Gimlet gin tonica

50 ml/1²/₃ oz. HMS Victory
   Navy Gin, or similar

20 ml/²/₃ oz. Rose's Lime Cordial

100 ml/3¹/₃ oz. chilled East
   Imperial Old World Tonic,
   or tonic water of your choice

100 ml/3¹/₃ oz. chilled soda or
   sparkling mineral water

lime wheels, to garnish

SERVES 1

This drink is inspired by elements of the Gimlet –
a cocktail comprising a mix of gin and lime cordial.

Half-fill a large balloon/copa glass (or large wine glass)
with ice cubes. Add the gin and lime cordial and stir.
Top up with tonic and soda, stir again and add a few
more ice cubes. Garnish with plenty of lime wheels
and serve at once.

Island daisy

120 ml/4 oz. gin

60 ml/2 oz. triple sec

60 ml/2 oz. freshly squeezed
   lime juice

2 tsp agave syrup

soda or sparkling mineral water,
   to top up

lime wedges, to garnish

SERVES 4

This version of the classic Margarita features gin
instead of tequila. It takes the drink back to the
original version that was called a Daisy. Keep
things old school, with triple sec for the citrusy
element, and top up with soda.

Chill 4 rocks glasses or tumblers in the freezer.

Combine the gin, triple sec, lime juice and agave syrup
in a cocktail shaker and add a handful of ice cubes.
Shake to mix. Pour into the chilled glasses, top up with
soda water (to taste), garnish each drink with a lime
wedge and serve at once.

Raspberry rickey

4 fresh raspberries

50 ml/1²/₃ oz. vodka

20 ml/²/₃ oz. freshly squeezed lime juice

1 tsp Chambord (black raspberry liqueur)

soda water, to top up

a lime wedge, to garnish

SERVES 1

This raspberry twist on a gin rickey is a fun, fruity drink with the perfect balance of sweet and tart – the perfect way to start your next long summer's evening spent in the garden.

Gently muddle the raspberries in the bottom of a highball glass. Fill the glass with ice cubes, add the remaining ingredients and stir gently. Garnish with a lime wedge and serve at once.

Berry caipiroska

4 lime wedges

a selection of fresh red berries (strawberries, raspberries and blueberries are all good), plus extra to garnish

2 white sugar cubes

50 ml/1²/₃ oz. vodka

an olive pick

SERVES 1

Fresh berries not only give this refreshing cocktail a sweet fruitiness, but they also make a delightfully pretty drink to serve at an alfresco summer lunch.

Add the lime wedges, 3–5 berries and the sugar cubes to a rocks glass. Muddle to extract the juice from the limes and crush the berries. Pour in the vodka, top up the glass with crushed ice and stir gently to mix.

Garnish with a selection of berries threaded onto an olive pick and serve at once.

Hugo

4 fresh mint leaves, plus a few extra to garnish

¼ lime, cut into wedges

25 ml/¾ oz. elderflower cordial

chilled Prosecco, to top up

a splash of soda water

SERVES 1

This combination of elderflower cordial and muddled fresh mint couldn't be more refreshing on a hot summer's day – for a virgin version, simply replace the Prosecco with a sparkling alcohol-free wine.

Put the mint leaves and the lime wedges in a large balloon/copa glass (or large wine glass) and gently muddle them. Add the elderflower cordial, a handful of ice cubes and half-fill the glass with Prosecco. Stir gently, top up with Prosecco and add a splash of soda water. Garnish with mint leaves and serve at once.

Nonna's garden

3 thick slices of cucumber, plus 1 fine slice to garnish

1 tsp freshly freshly squeezed lemon juice

1 tsp white sugar

4 fresh mint leaves, plus a few extra to garnish

chilled Prosecco, to top up

SERVES 1

The combination of cucumber and mint has such a refreshing aroma – it will cool you down even before you take your first sip! You can also try this recipe with fresh basil leaves instead of the mint.

Put the cucumber, lemon juice, sugar and mint leaves into a cocktail shaker and muddle well. Add a handful of ice cubes and shake vigorously. Strain into a large balloon/copa glass (or large wine glass) and top up with Prosecco. Garnish with a few mint leave and the fine cucumber slice and serve at once.

Sea breeze

—◦⋙◦—

30 ml/1 oz. vodka
150 ml/5 oz. cranberry juice
50 ml/1²⁄₃ oz. grapefruit juice
a lime wedge, to garnish

SERVES 1

A beach-themed party would be the perfect time to serve this classic concoction of grapefruit and cranberry juices with vodka. The flavours combine to create something new and delicious.

Half-fill a highball glass with ice cubes. Pour in the vodka and add the cranberry and grapefruit juices. Stir, garnish with a lime wedge and serve at once.

Moscow mule

—◦⋙◦—

50 ml/1²⁄₃ oz. vodka
4 lime wedges
chilled ginger beer, to top up

SERVES 1

A good ginger beer is what gives a mule its easy spiciness and it works beautifully here with zesty lime to create the perfect long drink for a hot summer's day.

Half-fill a highball glass with ice cubes. Pour in the vodka, squeeze over the lime wedges and drop the spent husks in too. Top up with ginger beer, stir and serve at once.

Bay breeze

175 ml/6 oz. golden rum
385 ml/13 oz. cranberry juice
175 ml/6 oz. pineapple juice
lime wedges, to garnish

SERVES 4

This totally tropical cocktail is simplicity itself to make, so ideal for larger gatherings too – just double up the ingredients, prepare the drink in advance and add ice cubes just before serving.

Add all the ingredients to a large jug/pitcher filled with ice cubes, stir and pour into 4 highball glasses filled with more ice cubes. Garnish each drink with a lime wedge and serve at once.

Tropical mojito

1 lime, cut into eight wedges
4 lychees in syrup, drained
   (or fresh if you can find them)
6 fresh mint sprigs
90 ml/3 oz. coconut white rum,
   such as Malibu
30 ml/1 oz. lychee liqueur
30 ml/1 oz. pineapple juice

SERVES 2

A twist on a classic mojito with coconut rum and lychee liqueur adding a taste of the tropics. Lychee liqueur is available online and made by brands including Monin, who make cocktail syrups.

Place the lime wedges, lychees and mint in a cocktail shaker and muddle well. Pour in the rum and lychee liqueur and add a handful of ice cubes. Shake vigorously and strain into 2 cocktail glasses. Add half the pineapple juice to each drink to top up and serve at once.

Bourbon spritz

20 ml/⅔ oz. Maker's 46 Bourbon, or similar

20 ml/⅔ oz. freshly squeezed pink grapefruit juice

10 ml/⅓ oz. Goji Berry Syrup (see page 9)

5 ml/1 tsp Campari

75 ml/2½ oz. chilled Prosecco

50 ml/1⅔ oz. chilled soda water

a fresh rosemary sprig and a grapefruit zest, to garnish

SERVES 1

Bright and fresh, this bourbon-based drink is the perfect pre-dinner tipple on a warm evening.

Half-fill a large wine glass with ice cubes. Pour in the bourbon, pink grapefruit juice, Goji Berry Syrup and Campari and stir for 5–10 seconds to combine and chill. Top up with the Prosecco and soda water and stir. Garnish with a rosemary sprig and a grapefruit zest and serve at once.

Marquee

45 ml/1½ oz. Maker's Mark Bourbon, or similar

45 ml/1½ oz. cranberry juice

15 ml/½ oz. Chambord (black raspberry liqueur)

15 ml/½ oz. freshly squeezed lemon juice

10 ml/⅓ oz. sugar syrup (see page 8)

3 fresh raspberries

10 ml/⅓ oz. egg white

a lemon zest and a raspberry, to garnish

SERVES 1

Here is proof that bourbon can work in long and fruity drinks too... This recipe was adapted from a cocktail created by Giovanni Burdi at Match Bar, London in 1998.

Combine all the ingredients in a cocktail shaker and 'dry' shake first (i.e. with no ice cubes), to emulsify the egg white. Add some ice cubes and shake again – hard this time – and strain into a highball glass, half-filled with ice cubes. Garnish with a lemon zest and a raspberry and serve at once.

Batanga 2

a lime wedge and sea salt flakes, to rim the glass

50 ml/1⅔ oz. Ocho Blanco tequila, or similar

25 ml/¾ oz. Amaro Averna liqueur

20 ml/⅔ oz. freshly squeezed lemon juice

25 ml/¾ oz. sugar syrup (see page 8)

a lime wheel, to garnish

SERVES 1

One of Mexico's most popular drinks, while the original Batanga recipe calls for tequila, lime, salt and Coca-Cola, this recipe foregoes cola and uses bitter Italian Amaro Averna to replicate its flavour.

Prepare a highball glass by rubbing the rim with a lime wedge, then dip the rim of the glass into the sea salt flakes. Pour all the ingredients into a cocktail shaker and add a handful of ice cubes. Shake for 12–15 seconds then double strain into the prepared glass, half-filled with ice cubes. Garnish with a lime wheel and serve at once.

El diablo

50 ml/1⅔ oz. Ocho Blanco tequila, or similar

25 ml/¾ oz. freshly squeezed lime juice

10 ml/⅓ oz. fresh ginger juice

20 ml/⅔ oz. sugar syrup (see page 8)

10 ml/⅓ oz. crème de cassis

chilled ginger ale, to top up

a lime wedge, to garnish

SERVES 1

This classic tequila drink was first featured in a cocktail book by legendary Tiki bar owner Trader Vic and listed as a 'Mexican El Diablo' ('Mexican Devil'), most likely because of the reddish hue the crème de cassis gives.

Add all the drink ingredients, except the ginger ale, to a cocktail shaker with a handful of ice cubes and shake hard. Strain into a highball glass and top up with ginger ale. Garnish with a lime wedge and serve at once.

Mint julep

8–10 fresh mint leaves, plus
3–4 extra sprigs to garnish

25 ml/³⁄₄ oz. sugar syrup
(see page 8)

75 ml/2¹⁄₂ oz. Michter's Bourbon,
or similar

SERVES 1

This Kentucky Derby mainstay originated in the American South in the 18th century. There are very few things as refreshing as sipping on this numbingly cold mixture of mint, sugar and bourbon churned with crushed ice on a hot summer's day. Be careful not to muddle the mint leaves too heavily, as this will make the drink bitter.

Combine the mint leaves and sugar syrup in a julep tin or tumbler and muddle gently to release the oils. Add the bourbon, then fill the tin up with crushed ice. Add all the ingredients and stir for about 30 seconds, until the outside of the tin is frosted. Cap the top of the drink with more crushed ice and garnish with mint sprigs. Add a straw and serve at once.

Bourbon cobbler

a pineapple slice, peeled

an orange slice

a lemon slice

50 ml/1²⁄₃ oz. bourbon

15 ml/¹⁄₂ oz. orange Curaçao

a fresh mint sprig, to garnish

SERVES 1

For a deliciously tropical alternative to a Mint Julep (above), try a refreshing Bourbon Cobbler.

Gently muddle the fruit in a rocks glass, add the bourbon, Curaçao and a few ice cubes and stir well. Add more ice cubes and stir again, garnish with a fresh mint sprig, add 2 short straws and serve at once.

Derby julep

1½ tsp runny honey

8 fresh mint leaves

60 ml/2 oz. Eagle Rare Bourbon, or similar

30 ml/1 oz. freshly squeezed pink grapefruit juice

5 ml/1 tsp orgeat (almond syrup)

a fresh mint sprig and pink grapefruit slices, to garnish

SERVES 1

This refreshing drink is a cross between a brown derby (bourbon, grapefruit and honey) and a classic Mint Julep (see page 58).

Combine the honey and mint leaves in the base of a highball glass. Muddle the mint very gently to release its oils. Add all the other ingredients and fill the glass with crushed ice. Stir together for about 20–30 seconds. Garnish the drink with a mint sprig and a pink grapefruit slice. Add a straw and serve at once.

Georgia mint julep

8 fresh mint leaves

2 dashes of Angostura bitters

25 ml/¾ oz. crème de pêche (peach liqueur)

75 ml/2½ oz. W.L. Weller 12 Year Old Bourbon, or similar

2–3 fresh mint sprigs, 2 fresh or frozen peach slices and icing/confectioners' sugar, to garnish

SERVES 1

Bourbon, mint and peach is another winning combination (even though the original recipe calls for brandy). For another variation, try substituting peach liqueur for an apricot brandy.

Combine the mint leaves, Angostura bitters and crème de pêche in a julep tin or tumbler and muddle gently to release the oils. Add the bourbon, then fill the tin with crushed ice. Stir the ingredients together for about 30 seconds, until the outside of the tin is frosted. Cap the top of the drink with crushed ice, garnish with mint sprigs and peach slices and dust lightly with icing/confectioners' sugar. Add a straw and serve at once.

Hibiscus highball

50 ml/1²⁄₃ oz. Cabeza tequila, or similar blanco tequila

25 ml/³⁄₄ oz. freshly squeezed lime juice

25 ml/³⁄₄ oz. hibiscus syrup (see page 9)

chilled soda water, to top up

an edible flower, to garnish (optional)

SERVES 1

Agua de jamaica (hibiscus water) is a popular non-alcoholic drink in Mexico. It also makes a good base for a beautifully refreshing tequila cocktail.

Half fill a highball glass with ice cubes. Add the tequila, lime juice and hibiscus syrup. Stir to mix and chill. Garnish with an edible flower (if using) and serve at once.

Matador

50 ml/1²⁄₃ fl oz. Ocho Blanco tequila, or similar blanco tequila

25 ml/³⁄₄ oz. freshly squeezed lime juice

30 ml/1 oz. pineapple juice

1½ tsp green Chartreuse

5 ml/1 tsp agave nectar

dehydrated pineapple and lime slices and freshly ground pink peppercorns, to garnish (optional)

SERVES 1

Here a classic cocktail has been 'upgraded' with the addition of green Chartreuse. Its herbaceous notes complement the tequila and fruity pineapple.

Pour the tequila, lime juice, pineapple juice, Chartreuse and agave nectar into a cocktail shaker and add a handful of ice cubes. Shake and strain into a highball glass. Garnish the drink with dehydrated pineapple and lime slices and a grinding of pink peppercorns, if using, and serve at once.

Anejo highball

50 ml/1²⁄₃ oz. aged rum

15 ml/½ oz. orange Curaçao

15 ml/½ oz. freshly squeezed lime juice

2 dashes of Angostura bitters

chilled ginger beer, to top up

an orange zest spiral, to garnish

SERVES 1

'Rum, lime and curaçao are the holy trinity of Caribbean cocktails.' So says legendary American bartender Dale de Groff, the creator of this tribute to the classic drinks created in Cuba.

Fill a highball glass with ice cubes and add the rum, Curaçao, lime juice and Angostura bitters. Top up with ginger beer and stir gently to mix. Garnish with an orange zest spiral and serve at once.

Planter's punch

50 ml/1²⁄₃ oz. light Puerto Rican-style rum

50 ml/1²⁄₃ oz. freshly squeezed orange juice

30 ml/1 oz. freshly squeezed lemon juice

15 ml/½ oz. grenadine

25 ml/¾ oz. chilled soda water

10 ml/⅓ oz. dark Jamaican rum

an orange slice and a cocktail cherry, to garnish

SERVES 1

As the title itself suggests, a Planter's Punch was the house punch consumed on Caribbean plantations. As a result, there aren't really any hard or fast rules as to what to include so long as you stick to the punch mantra of sour, sweet, strong and weak, but here is a delicious recipe.

Add the light rum, orange and lemon juices and grenadine to a cocktail shaker and shake together. Pour into a highball glass filled with crushed ice and top up with the soda. Gently pour the dark rum over the surface of the drink – it should float naturally on top. Garnish with an orange slice and a cocktail cherry and serve at once.

Hedgerow sling

25 ml/¾ oz. gin

25 ml/¾ oz. sloe gin

25 ml/¾ oz. freshly squeezed lemon juice

10 ml/⅓ oz. sugar syrup (see page 8)

100 ml/3⅓ oz. soda water

10 ml/⅓ oz. crème de mure

a fresh strawberry and a lemon slice, to garnish

SERVES 1

Here's a cocktail that with the right amount of care can look as good as it tastes. Drizzle the crème de mure gently into the drink, right at the end, to create a beautiful marbled effect.

Add the gin, sloe gin, lemon juice and sugar syrup to a cocktail shaker filled with ice cubes and shake. Strain into a sling or highball glass filled with crushed ice. Top up with the soda water and slowly drizzle over the crème de mure. Garnish with a strawberry and a slice of lemon and serve at once.

Singapore sling

25 ml/¾ oz. gin

25 ml/¾ oz. cherry brandy

10 ml/⅓ oz. Benedictine

25 ml/¾ oz. freshly squeezed lemon juice

a small dash of Angostura bitters

soda water, to top up

a lemon zest curl and a cocktail cherry, to garnish

SERVES 1

Created at the Long Bar at Raffles Hotel in Singapore, when this drink is made correctly, and without using one of the cheap pre-mixes that are so prevalent today, it is the peak of sophistication. The original recipe has long been a subject of hot debate; this version is perhaps one of the best...

Put all the ingredients in a mixing beaker (or similar) filled with ice cubes and stir gently to mix. Fill a sling or highball glass with ice cubes, pour in the drink and top up with soda water. Garnish with a lemon zest curl and a cocktail cherry and serve at once.

Slushies & Floats

Mint julep slushie

100 g/scant ½ cup white sugar

6 fresh mint sprigs, plus extra
  to garnish

60–80 ml/2–2¾ oz. bourbon

SERVES 2

There are very few things as refreshing as this
lip-tingling mixture of mint, sugar and bourbon
churned with crushed ice on a hot summer's day.

Place 160 ml/5½ oz. water in a saucepan with the sugar
and mint and bring to the boil. Turn down the heat and
simmer for about 5 minutes, swirling the pan a little, until
you have a thin syrup. Remove from the heat and leave to
cool completely. Strain, transfer to a small jug/pitcher and
chill in the fridge. Fill 2 highball glasses with crushed ice.
Divide the mint syrup between them, follow with the
bourbon and stir well. Garnish each drink with a mint
sprig, add straws and serve at once.

Sea breeze slushie

125 ml/4 oz. vodka

125 ml/4 oz. cranberry juice

60 ml/2 oz. grapefruit juice

TO SERVE

200 ml/6¾ oz. cranberry juice

2 tbsp grenadine

60 ml/2 oz. vodka

a freezerproof lidded container

SERVES 2

Tangy grapefruit and cranberry juices work so
well served as an icy slushie – a cocktail umbrella
to serve is optional! (See photo on page 68.)

Mix together the vodka, cranberry juice and grapefruit
juice in a lidded freezerproof container. Cover with the
lid and freeze overnight. To serve, remove the container
from the freezer and crush the contents with a fork
to create a slushie texture. Divide the cranberry juice
between 2 hurricane or coupe glasses and add half the
grenadine and vodka to each. Add a large spoonful of the
frozen slushie to each glass, add straws and serve at once.

Firecracker popsicle slushie

The famous American firecracker popsicles are very patriotic with their red, white and blue stripes, flavoured with cherry, lemonade and blue raspberry. Why not try this delicious and vibrant homemade slushie version?

FOR THE BLUE RASPBERRY SLUSHIE

30 ml/1 oz. blue curaçao

30 ml/1 oz. Chambord (black raspberry liqueur) or similar

100 ml/3⅓ oz. vodka

100 ml/3⅓ oz. clear sparkling lemonade

FOR THE LEMONADE SLUSHIE

125 ml/4 oz. vodka

180 ml/6 oz. clear sparkling lemonade

freshly squeezed juice of 1 lemon

FOR THE CHERRY SLUSHIE

125 ml/4 oz. vodka

180 ml/6 oz. cherry juice

TO SERVE

fresh strawberries, to garnish

3 freezerproof lidded containers

SERVES 2–3

Mix together the liquids for each of the slushie flavours in 3 separate bowls. Transfer the mixtures to 3 separate lidded freezerproof containers. Cover with the lids and freeze overnight.

To serve, remove the containers from the freezer and use a fork to crush and break up their contents to create a slushie texture.

Assemble the drinks by using a spoon to carefully layer up each of the 3 mixtures in equal quantities in hurricane or highball glasses. Start with the blue raspberry, then add the lemonade layer and finish with the red cherry. Garnish each drink with a strawberry slice, add straws and serve at once.

Blueberry bubble slushie

Taiwanese bubble tea, the popular drink, is the inspiration for this slushie. Bubble tea is traditionally made with tapioca pearls, but in this recipe uses blueberry and lemon flavour bursting juice bubbles. They make a vibrant garnish on top of this boozy slushie.

200 g/7 oz. fresh blueberries, plus 12 extra to garnish

60 g/¼ cup white sugar

freshly squeezed juice of 1 lemon

60 ml/2 oz. vodka

2 tbsp blueberry- and lemon-flavoured bursting juice bubbles, such as Popaballs

2 long lemon zest strips, to garnish

2 olive picks

SERVES 2

Put the blueberries, sugar and lemon juice in a small saucepan with 120 ml/4 oz. cold water and bring to a simmer over a gentle heat for about 5–10 minutes, until the fruit is soft. Pass the fruit through a sieve/strainer over a jug/pitcher, pressing down with a spoon to release as much juice as possible. Discard any skins or pulp that remain in the sieve/strainer. Leave to cool completely.

Prepare the garnishes in advance by threading 6 fresh blueberries and 1 lemon zest strip onto each of 2 olive picks as shown. Set aside.

To serve, fill 2 highball glasses with crushed ice. Add half the blueberry syrup mixture and half the vodka to each glass and stir gently. Top each drink with a spoonful of bursting juice bubbles, garnish with a prepared fruit pick, and serve at once with fat straws to slurp up the bubbles.

Piña colada slushie

Conjuring up scenes of beaches with palm trees overhead, the Piña Colada cocktail is best enjoyed when lying on a sunlounger. Sadly, this is not always possible – but serving this slushie at home may help transport your mind to sunnier climes. For a totally tropical feel, use hollowed out coconuts or pineapples as serving vessels. If you want to make the slushie boozier, add a little more rum with the extra pineapple juice.

125 ml/4 oz. coconut milk

125 ml/4 oz. white coconut rum such as Malibu

60 ml/2 oz. vodka

375 ml/13 oz. pineapple juice, plus an extra 200 ml/6¾ oz. to serve (though you may not need all of this)

cocktail cherries, pineapple wedges and pineapple leaves, to garnish

a freezerproof lidded container

SERVES 2

Mix the coconut milk well to get rid of any large clumps that sometimes form at the top of the can. In the lidded freezerproof container, whisk together the coconut milk, rum, vodka and pineapple juice until well blended. Cover the container with the lid and freeze overnight.

When you are ready to serve, remove the container from the freezer. Do not worry if the mixture has separated. Using a fork, crush the mixture into small ice crystals. It should only be semi-frozen due to the vodka and easy to crush. Add the extra pineapple juice slowly and mix to make a loose slushie consistency – you might not need all of the juice.

Divide the slushie between 2 hurricane or highball glasses or pineapple/coconut shells. Garnish each drink with a cocktail cherry and a pineapple wedge, add straws and serve at once.

Sgroppino

Equally at home as a drink, served as a refreshing summer dessert or even a palate-cleanser between courses, this classic Italian frozen cocktail is probably the most gorgeous slushie you'll ever encounter. Why not keep a tub of lemon sorbet in your freezer and a few individual-serving size bottles of fizz in your fridge for when the urge for a Sgroppino takes hold!

60 ml/2 oz. vodka

2 rounded tbsp lemon sorbet

2 dashes of egg white (optional though it's a good addition as it makes the drink more frothy)

2 x 200-ml/6¾-oz. (small) bottles chilled Prosecco, Asti Spumante or other sparkling white wine

finely grated lemon zest, to garnish

SERVES 2

If you have time, put the vodka and a mixing bowl (ideally metal) in the freezer for a few hours before you want to serve the drinks.

Put the vodka, lemon sorbet, egg white (if using) in the freezer-frosted bowl and add 1 bottle of the Prosecco. Using a ballon whisk, beat well to combine and introduce air into the mixture.

Carefully spoon the mixture into 2 chilled coupes, cocktail glasses or Champagne flutes. Top up with the second bottle of Prosecco (you may not need all of it) and stir very gently. Garnish each drink with a sprinkle of lemon zest, add a spoon or a straw (depending on what is most practical for your choice of glassware) and serve at once.

West coast sunset

1 x 500-ml/1-pint tub mango
  sorbet (you will need
  1 large scoop per serving)

2 tsp grenadine or strawberry
  syrup (see page 8)

chilled sparkling rosé wine, to top
  up (a fruity Italian Rosato
  Frizzante works well)

freshly squeezed lime or orange
  juice, to taste

SERVES 1

Not so much a cocktail as theatre – this is all
about the fun of recreating the visual spectacle of
a beautiful pink and orange evening sky in a glass.

Remove the mango sorbet from the freezer 10 minutes
before assembling the drink to allow it to soften. Pour
the grenadine or syrup into a large cocktail glass or coupe.
Using an ice cream scoop, add a nice round ball of mango
sorbet to the glass. Top up with sparkling wine and add
a squeeze of fresh lime or orange juice just to season.
Serve at once with a small spoon.

Sgroppinko

about 8 rounded tsp lemon sorbet

60 ml/2 oz. pink gin (ideally a
  fruity, red-berry flavoured one)

chilled sparkling rosé wine, to
  top up (a fruity Italian Rosato
  Frizzante works well)

fresh raspberries and finely grated
  lemon zest, to garnish

SERVES 2

This variation on the classic Italian Sgroppino
(see page 79) is a delicious blend of raspberry
sorbet, Prosecco and pink gin. Serve in place of
a dessert for a zesty end to a summer meal.

Remove the sorbet from the freezer 10 minutes before you
want to make the drink to allow it to soften. Using a
melon baller, add 4 small scoops of sorbet to each of
2 highball glasses. Add the gin and top up with sparkling
wine. Garnish each drink for a few raspberries and a
sprinkle of lemon zest, add a straw and serve at once.

Twisted pineapple frosé

If a Hawaiian luau is your idea of the ultimate summer party, then here is a tropical take on a Classic Strawberry Frosé (see page 88), perfect for the next time you plan to have some serious fun in the sun.

1 x 750-ml/25-oz. bottle dark pink, full-bodied rosé wine (a Pinot Noir or Merlot works well)

250 ml/1 cup pineapple juice

45 ml/1½ oz. Bacardi, or other white rum

30 ml/1 oz. sugar syrup (see page 8)

30 ml/1 oz. freshly squeezed lime juice

½ a fresh red chilli/chile, deseeded and finely chopped, plus extra to garnish (optional)

a pineapple leaf and/or pineapple wedge, to garnish

a freezerproof lidded container

SERVES 4

Pour the rosé wine and pineapple juice into a lidded freezerproof container. Stir to mix, add the lid and freeze until solid. Remove from the freezer and allow it to defrost for about 35–40 minutes, until you can break it up with a fork but it's still holding plenty of ice crystals.

Scoop into the cup of a blender and add the Bacardi, sugar syrup, lime juice and chilli/chile. Blend for about 30 seconds until foamy and speckled with red chilli/chile.

Spoon into 4 coupes or cocktail glasses, add a pineapple leaf and/or a pineapple wedge and a sprinkling of red chilli/chile to garnish (optional). Add straws and serve at once with small spoons as well.

Watermelon, lime & mint frosé

Here's how to survive the next heatwave. Get some booze in the blender and serve up this tooth-tingling and absurdly refreshing adults-only frozen treat.

60 ml/2 oz. watermelon and rosé syrup (see page 9)

250 ml/1 cup fresh watermelon juice (see below)

1 x 750-ml/25-oz. bottle full-flavoured, full-bodied rosé wine (a Pinot Noir or Merlot works well here)

45 ml/1½ oz. freshly squeezed lime juice

30 ml/1 oz. vodka

5–6 fresh mint leaves

watermelon balls, finely grated lime zest and lime wheels, to garnish

FOR THE FRESH WATERMELON JUICE

500 g/1 lb. fresh watermelon flesh, deseeded and cubed

a freezerproof lidded container

SERVES 4

Make the watermelon and rosé syrup as directed on page 9 and set aside to cool.

To make fresh watermelon juice, put the watermelon cubes in a blender and blend until puréed. Strain the liquid through a sieve/strainer into a jug/pitcher. Discard the fruit pulp and any seeds. Reserve the juice to use as directed below.

To make the frosé mixture, pour the rosé wine and 250 ml/1 cup of the fresh watermelon juice into a lidded freezerproof container. Stir to mix, then cover with the lid and freeze until solid. Remove from the freezer about 35–40 minutes before you want to make the drinks. It needs to have defrosted enough for you to be able to break it up with a fork but it should still be holding plenty of ice crystals.

Scoop the frosé mixture into the cup of a blender and add the watermelon and rosé syrup, lime juice, vodka and mint. Blend for about 30 seconds until pale pink and foamy and speckled with green mint. Pour into 4 coupes, garnish with watermelon balls, lime wheels and lime zests. Add straws and serve at once.

Gin tonica float

The ice-cream float is a childhood favourite and tastes as good today as it did back then. This gin and tonic variant uses lemon sorbet for a more tart flavour, but has a similar effect to the ice cream in a float. The point of perfection with this drink is when the sorbet starts to melt and you suck little bits of it up through the straw. It is indulgent, but a lighter alternative to a dessert. You can try it with different flavours too – blood orange sorbet adds an extra zing, whilst blackcurrant sorbet would add more tartness. You could even use Champagne sorbet for a summer celebration.

1 large scoop of lemon sorbet, or sorbet flavour of your choice (see introduction)

50 ml/1²⁄₃ oz. Beefeater Gin, or similar

150 ml/5 oz. chilled London Essence Co. Classic London Tonic Water, or tonic water of your choice

finely pared lemon peel strips, to garnish

SERVES 1

Remove the sorbet from the freezer 10 minutes before you want to make the drink to allow it to soften.

Combine the gin and tonic in a large large balloon/copa glass (or large wine glass). Add a scoop of lemon sorbet to the glass, being sure that it doesn't fizz up and cause the drink to overflow.

Garnish with lemon peel strips, add a straw and serve at once with a small spoon.

Classic strawberry frosé

Nothing beats a frosted glass of rosé wine on a summer's day, except perhaps this ice-blended frosé! Taking just a little time to make the strawberry syrup pays off as your rosé will lose some oomph during freezing so this addition boosts both the fruity flavour and pink hue of the drink.

1 x 750-ml/25-oz. bottle dark pink, full-bodied rosé wine (a Pinot Noir or Merlot works well)

100 ml/3⅓ oz. strawberry syrup (see page 8)

45 ml/1½ oz. freshly squeezed lemon juice

finely pared lemon zest, to garnish

a freezerproof lidded container

SERVES 3–4

Pour the rosé wine into a lidded freezerproof container, add the lid and transfer to the freezer. Leave until almost frozen, about 4–5 hours.

When you are ready to serve, remove the container from the freezer and scrape the frozen rosé into the cup of a blender. Add the strawberry syrup, lemon juice and a large scoop of crushed ice. Blend until smooth.

Pour the mixture back into the freezerproof container and return it to the freezer for about 35–40 minutes, just until the mixture is thickened but you can easily break up the crystals with a fork. Spoon into hurricane or highball glasses, garnish with the lemon zest, add straws and serve at once.

Dark & stormy float

A Dark & Stormy is a classic rum cocktail. With an added few scoops
of clever cheat's ginger and lime ice cream, summer just got cooler. (This recipe
makes more ice cream than you need for one serving of this float but
it will keep in the freezer for another time.)

**500 ml/1 pint store-bought
vanilla ice cream**

**2 pieces of stem ginger in syrup
from a jar, finely chopped,
plus extra to garnish**

**4 tbsp syrup from the jar
of stem ginger (see above)**

**finely grated zest and freshly
squeezed juice of 4 limes,
plus extra zest to garnish**

50 ml/1²/₃ oz. dark rum

**275 ml/1 cup plus 1 tbsp
ginger beer**

2 tsp ground ginger

*a freezerproof lidded container
(optional)*

SERVES 1

Remove the vanilla ice cream from the freezer and allow
it to soften for about 10–15 minutes. Tip it into a mixing
bowl and fold in the chopped stem ginger, ginger syrup
and the zest and juice of the limes. Scoop back into the
tub (or a freezerproof container if easier) and pop it back
into the freezer for a few minutes. Put a milkshake glass
into the freezer at the same time to chill.

When you are ready to serve, place a scoop of ginger
and lime ice cream at the bottom of the freezer-frosted
glass before adding the rum and half of the ginger beer.
Once the foam stops rising, add another scoop of ice
cream before adding the remaining ginger beer. Top with
an extra scoop of ice cream if you want to, garnish with
a sprinkle of chopped stem ginger and lime zest. Add a
straw and serve at once with a spoon.

Raspberry ripple float

4 scoops of store-bought raspberry ripple ice cream, or similar

10 fresh raspberries

500 ml/17 oz. chilled raspberry or cherry soda, as preferred

pink sprinkles, to garnish

SERVES 2

Relive your memories of innocent childhood summers with this sweet raspberry ripple ice cream soda that's sure to float your nostalgic boat.

Put 1 scoop of ice cream in the bottom of each of 2 milkshake glasses and divide the fresh raspberries between them. Top up the glasses with raspberry or cherry soda and finish with a second scoop of ice cream. Garnish with a few sprinkles, add straws and serve at once.

Spiced almond horchata float

140 g/1 cup blanched raw almonds

2 tbsp brown sugar

1 tsp ground cinnamon, plus extra to garnish

125 ml/4½ oz. dark rum (optional)

4 scoops of store-bought vanilla ice cream, or another flavour of your choice (try chocolate or salted caramel)

SERVES 4

These floats are a really fun way to end a summer barbecue/cookout. They are refreshing and not too heavy and you can serve them as a dessert.

Soak the almonds in water for 6–24 hours. Strain the almonds and place in a blender with 500 ml/2 cups cold water. Add the sugar, cinnamon and rum (if using) and blend until smooth. Pour into a large pitcher/jug filled with ice cubes. Fill 4 highball glasses with crushed ice and pour in the horchata, leaving a space of 2.5 cm/1 inch at the rim. Top each drink with a scoop of ice cream and dust with cinnamon. Add straws and serve at once with spoons.

Punches
& Pitchers

Rose-tinted spectacles

250 ml/1 cup Absolut Citron vodka, or similar

250 ml/1 cup Absolut Kurant vodka, or similar

2 litres/2 quarts clear apple juice

50 ml/1²/₃ oz. sugar syrup (see page 8)

1 tsp Angostura bitters

60 ml/2 oz. freshly squeezed lime juice

lemon or lime slices, to garnish

SERVES 10

Here zingy blackcurrant- and citrus-flavoured vodkas combine with apple juice for a light and refreshing summer cocktail that is easily batched up to make a pitcher. Absolut is the iconic brand but you can easily substitute other vodkas..

Add all the ingredients to a large jug/pitcher filled with ice cubes and stir gently to mix.

Pour into ice-filled highball glasses, garnish with lemon or lime slices and serve at once.

Pimm's deluxe

400 ml/1³/₄ cups Pimm's No. 1

50 ml/1²/₃ oz. elderflower cordial

1 x 750-ml/25-oz. bottle Prosecco, chilled

orange, lemon and cucumber slices, hulled strawberries and fresh mint sprigs, to garnish

SERVES 6

Once you've tried this you'll wonder why you haven't been adding Prosecco to Pimm's all your life! However it is best to keep in mind that it packs more of a punch than your regular Pimm's and lemonade. (See photo on page 94.)

Add the Pimm's and elderflower cordial to a large jug/pitcher filled with ice cubes and stir gently to mix. Add the sliced fruit and strawberries and pour in the Prosecco.

Divide the mixture between 6 ice-filled highball glasses, sliding a little fruit into each one. Garnish each drink with a mint sprig and serve at once.

Primavera punch

50 ml/1²/₃ oz. blanco tequila

25 ml/³/₄ oz. freshly squeezed lime juice

25 ml/³/₄ oz. raspberry syrup (see page 9)

chilled Champagne or other dry sparkling white wine, to top up

fresh mint sprigs and a fresh raspberry, to garnish

SERVES 1

This punch is dangerously drinkable. Raspberries, tequila and Champagne – what's not to love? But probably best served with some cocktail nibbles...

Add the tequila, lime juice and raspberry syrup to a cocktail shaker and add a handful of ice cubes. Shake and strain into an ice-filled highball glass. Top up with Champagne, garnish with a mint sprig and a raspberry and serve at once.

Hurricane

50 ml dark Jamaican rum

25 ml/1²/₃ oz. freshly squeezed lemon juice

25 ml/1²/₃ oz. passion fruit syrup (store-bought is fine here)

passion fruit juice, to top up (optional)

a cocktail cherry and an orange slice, to garnish

SERVES 1

Do not be tempted to use the hurricane mix widely available but instead play with different brands of bottled passion fruit syrup. You may want to add a splash of passion fruit juice too, if you want to make this drink feel like it's lasting longer.

Add all the ingredients to a cocktail shaker and add a handful of ice cubes. Shake vigorously and strain into a hurricane glass or Tiki mug filled with crushed ice. Top up with passion fruit juice (if using), garnish with a cocktail cherry and an orange slice and serve at once

Pomegranate punch

500 ml/2 cups vodka

750 ml/3 cups pomegranate juice

freshly squeezed juice of
  5 pink grapefruits

freshly squeezed juice of 8 limes

150 ml/5 oz. sugar syrup
  (see page 8)

500 ml/2 cups chilled soda water

long strips of grapefruit zest and
  fresh mint sprigs, to garnish

SERVES 10

This pink punch is as delicious to drink as it is to look at! Cut fine strips of grapefruit zest and add them to the glasses before pouring the drink.

Put the vodka, pomegranate, grapefruit and lime juices, and the sugar syrup in a large jug/pitcher filled with ice cubes. Top up with the soda water and stir gently to mix. Pour into ice-filled highball glasses, already garnished with a grapefruit zest spiral as shown, add a mint sprig and serve at once.

Pineapple pisco punch

1 x 700 ml/23-oz. bottle Pisco

500 ml/2 cups pineapple syrup
  (see page 9)

freshly squeezed juice of 9 lemons

500 ml/2 cups chilled soda water

fresh pineapple wedges, to garnish

SERVES 10

This delightfully refreshing punch is a variation on the classic Pisco Sour (see page 29) with the addition of a delicious homemade pineapple syrup.

Add the Pisco, pineapple syrup, lemon juice and soda water to a large jug/pitcher filled with ice cubes and stir gently to mix.

Pour into ice-filled highball glasses, garnish each drink with a pineapple wedge and serve at once.

Just peachy punch

A pale pink Provençal rosé wine, peach purée and French brandy come together here with delicious results.

4 ripe peaches, pitted and cut into wedges

75 ml/2½ fl. oz. brandy

75 ml/2½ fl. oz. peach schnapps

1 x 750-ml/25-oz. bottle dry, crisp rosé wine, chilled

375 ml/1½ cups peach juice/nectar or purée (see Note)

1–1½ litres/4–6 cups chilled Indian tonic water

peach slices and fresh basil sprigs, to garnish

SERVES 6–8

Put the peaches in a large jug/pitcher, pour over the brandy and schnapps and leave to marinate for a few hours.

When ready to serve, add the wine to the jug/pitcher along with the peach juice/nectar and add plenty of ice cubes. Stir and top up with tonic. Pour into ice-filled tumblers, garnish each drink with a peach slice and a sprig of basil and serve at once.

Note: If you can't find bottled peach juice or purée, blend about 6 stoned/pitted ripe peaches (to yield 375 ml/1½ cups of juice) and pass the purée through a sieve/strainer to remove any fibre or lumps. Taste and sweeten to taste if necessary with a little sugar syrup before using. It will depend on the ripeness of the peaches used.

Spicy ginger & berry cooler

Here is a super-simple punch that requires the minimum of effort but tastes delicious nonetheless, whilst being lower in alcohol than many punch recipes as it contains no spirits. It needs to sit in the fridge for a few hours to allow the fruit to macerate in the wine and add flavour. The hint of spice from the ginger ale adds the perfect finishing touch.

1 x 750-ml/25-oz. bottle fruity and sweet rosé wine, chilled

100 g/1 cup fresh strawberries, hulled and sliced

100 g/1 cup fresh raspberries

50 g/¼ cup white sugar

1 litre/4 cups chilled ginger ale

orange slices, to garnish

SERVES 6–8

Pour the wine into a large jug/pitcher and add the strawberries, raspberries and sugar. Cover and marinate for a few hours in the fridge.

When ready to serve, add the ginger ale to the jug/pitcher and gently stir. Add ice cubes and pour into ice-filled tumblers. Spoon a few of the wine-marinated berries into each drink, garnish with orange slices and serve at once.

Cherry vanilla kiss

125 ml/½ cup white sugar

400 g/2 cups fresh cherries, pitted

1 vanilla pod/bean, whole

1 x 750-ml/25-oz. bottle fruity and sweet rosé wine, chilled

125 ml/½ cup brandy

125 ml/½ cup Morello cherry cordial

65 ml/¼ cup cherry bitters

500 ml/2 cups chilled soda water

vanilla pods/beans, to garnish (optional)

SERVES 8

A cotton-candy inspired sweet treat for those with a passion for all things cherry.

Bring 125 ml/½ cup water and the sugar to a simmer in a small saucepan and stir until the sugar has just dissolved. Remove from the heat. Put the cherries and vanilla pod/bean into a large jug/pitcher, pour in the warm syrup and let stand for 5 minutes. Add the wine, brandy, cherry cordial and cherry bitters and stir to combine. Chill for at least 1 hour. When ready to serve, add the soda and pour into ice-filled highball glasses. Garnish each serving with a vanilla pod/bean (if using) and serve at once.

Tutti frutti

1 x 750-ml/25-oz. bottle rosé wine

8 fresh cherries, pitted

8 fresh strawberries, hulled

2 white peaches, pitted and sliced

2 tbsp white sugar

225 ml/8 oz. vodka

225 ml/8 oz. fresh watermelon juice (see page 84)

freshly squeezed juice of 1 lime

1 x 750-ml/25-oz. bottle medium white wine, chilled

cherries and lime slices, to garnish

SERVES 8

Full of juicy summer fruits, this drink is as pretty as a picture! You'll need to use a dark, fruity and very sweet rosé for the pink ice cubes.

First make the rosé wine ice cubes. Pour the rosé wine into ice cube trays and transfer to the freezer. Meanwhile, combine all the other ingredients, except the white wine, in a large jug/pitcher. Leave for at least 2 hours.

When ready to serve, add the white wine to the jug/pitcher and gently stir. Pour into rocks glasses or tumblers half-filled with the pink ice cubes. Garnish each drink with a cherry and a lime slice and serve at once.

Sparkling Mediterranean punch

The scent of fresh thyme will transport you to a village nestled away on a hilltop in Tuscany. This recipe makes an extra-large quantity so it is ideal for an alfresco summer party. You'll need a 3.5-litre/scant 4 quart capacity punch bowl or even a 'lemonade dispenser' with a tap to serve.

4 sprigs of fresh thyme, plus extra to garnish

1 x 750-ml/25-oz. bottle Aperol, chilled

1 x 750-ml/25-oz. bottle Lillet, or dry vermouth, chilled

1 litre/4 cups fresh pink grapefruit juice

1 x 750-ml/25-oz. bottle sparkling rosé wine (a Cava Rosada or rosé Prosecco both work well), chilled

pink grapefruit slices, to garnish

SERVES 20

Combine the thyme sprigs, Aperol, vermouth and grapefruit juice in a very large jug/pitcher or bowl and chill for at least 2 hours.

Add the sparkling rosé wine and plenty of ice cubes. Add a few ice cubes and a slice of grapefruit to each serving glass – small wine glasses, rocks glasses or tumblers can be used. Pour in the punch, add a sprig of fresh thyme to each drink to garnish and serve at once.

White sangria

1 x 750-ml/25-oz. bottle crisp dry white wine, chilled

100 ml/3⅓ oz. St. Germain elderflower liqueur

100 ml/3⅓ oz. dry vermouth

100 ml/3⅓ oz. Cointreau

freshly squeezed juice of 2 lemons

30 ml/1 oz. sugar syrup (see page 8)

2 dashes of grapefruit bitters

sliced fresh fruit, such as green seedless grapes, kiwi fruits, peaches or nectarines, to garnish

SERVES 10

St. Germain elderflower liqueur adds a wonderful floral note to this twist on a classic sangria and brings out the sweetness of the season's fruits.

Add all the ingredients to a large jug/pitcher filled with ice cubes and stir gently to mix.

Pour into ice-filled rocks glasses or tumblers, garnish with the fruit and serve at once.

Classic sangria

1 x 750-ml/25-oz. bottle red wine, chilled

150 ml/5 oz. Grand Marnier

250 ml/1 cup freshly squeezed orange juice

50 ml/1⅔ oz. sugar syrup (see page 8)

3 dashes of Angostura bitters

sliced fresh fruit, such as strawberries, apples, oranges and lemons, to garnish

SERVES 10

Everyone needs to know how to make a good Sangria, the good news is that there are very few rules. So long as you add red wine (a Spanish Rioja is especially good) and some fresh seasonal fruit, you shouldn't disappoint anyone!

Add all the ingredients to a large jug/pitcher filled with ice cubes and stir gently to mix.

Pour into ice-filled rocks glasses or tumblers, garnish each drink with a variety of fruit and serve at once.

Bellini rum punch

2 ripe peaches, skin on

40 ml/1⅓ oz. freshly squeezed lemon juice

60 ml/2 oz. peach schnapps

120 ml/4 oz. golden or white rum

120 ml/4 oz. white peach juice

1 x 750-ml/25-oz. bottle Prosecco, chilled

SERVES 4

This peachy little number will get the party started. Use a golden rum for this punch for the best flavour, but white rum if you can't find it.

Thinly slice the peaches and put them in a jug/pitcher. Add the lemon juice, schnapps, rum and peach juice and stir well. Add a handful of ice cubes, pour in the Prosecco and stir very gently. Pour into ice-filled highball glasses, sliding in a few peach slices, and serve at once.

La rossa

8 fresh strawberries

2 tsp white sugar

60 ml/2 oz. limoncello

2 tsp strawberry bursting juice bubbles (optional), see page 75

chilled Prosecco, to top up

SERVES 2

Summer in a glass. All you need now is a warm day, a flower-filled meadow, a picnic and someone lovely to share it with...

Hull 6 of the strawberries and chop them. Put them in a cocktail shaker with the sugar and muddle until the juices are released. Add the limoncello and a handful of ice cubes and shake. Strain into 2 chilled Champagne flutes. Add the bursting juice bubbles (if using). Half-fill the glasses with Prosecco, stir, and top up with more Prosecco. Slice the remaining strawberries, use to garnish the drinks and serve at once.

Prosecco iced tea

1 Earl Grey tea bag

1 tbsp white sugar

30 ml/1 oz. gin

1 tsp freshly squeezed lemon juice

a few dashes of elderflower cordial

chilled Prosecco, to top up

lemon slices, to garnish

SERVES 1

Tea, gin and Prosecco: all your favourite summer refreshments in one glass! Heaven. Next time you fancy a Long Island Iced Tea, think again… and try this far more elegant drink instead.

First, make an infusion by putting the tea bag and sugar in a cup and pouring over 75 ml/2½ oz. boiling water, then leave for 5 minutes. Remove the tea bag and leave to cool to room temperature.

Pour the Earl Grey infusion into a highball glass and add the gin, lemon juice and elderflower cordial. Add plenty of ice cubes and stir well to chill. Top up with Prosecco, garnish with lemon slices and serve at once.

Berry collins

125 ml/½ cup puréed red berries (blitz them in a blender and force through a sieve/strainer)

125 ml/½ cup sugar syrup (see page 8)

500 ml/2 cups London dry gin

freshly squeezed juice of 6 lemons

1 litre/4 cups chilled soda water

fresh red berries, to garnish

SERVES 10

The Tom Collins is a cocktail-party classic but scaled up and with the addition of a berry purée it works well as a summer punch. You can use mixed frozen berries to make your purée.

Add all the ingredients except the soda water to a large jug/pitcher filled with ice cubes and stir gently to mix. Top up with the soda water and stir again.

Pour into ice-filled highball glasses, garnish each drink with a few fresh berries and serve at once.

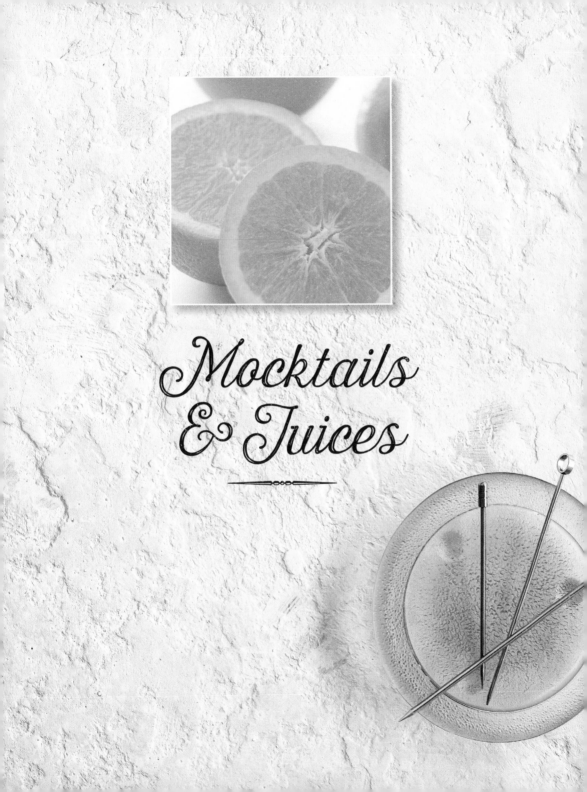

Mocktails & Juices

Raspberry, apple & lychee juice

200 g/1½ cups frozen raspberries

565 g/4⅓ cups canned lychees, drained

250 ml/1 cup clear apple juice

SERVES 2

Rehydrate with this juicily delectable drink. Using frozen raspberries keeps the drink ice-cold for ultimate refreshment on a hot summer's day. Healthy just got a whole lot tastier!

Simply put all the ingredients in a blender and blend until smooth. Pour into 2 highball glasses and serve at once.

Orange sunset

6 oranges

2 pomegranates

SERVES 2

This vibrant and deliciously tangy juice is reminiscent of the classic Tequila Sunrise cocktail, with the beautiful colours of the orange and pomegranate evoking the early evening sun.

Peel the oranges, chop the flesh and press it through an electric juicer into a jug/pitcher. Half the pomegranates and using a lemon squeezer, squeeze out the juice into a separate jug/pitcher.

Pour the orange juice into the 2 ice-filled highball glasses or tumblers then pour in the pomegranate juice in a thin stream – do not stir. Serve at once.

Shirley Temple

25 ml/¾ oz. grenadine or use any flavoured syrup of your choice (see pages 8–9)

ginger ale or clear sparkling lemonade, to top up

a lemon wedge, to garnish

SERVES 1

This sweet thirstquencher is perhaps the best known 'mocktail' and has been around for years but for good reason – it's simple and delicious! Try it with any of the flavoured syrups on pages 8–9.

Pour the grenadine into an ice-filled highball glass and top up with either ginger ale or lemonade. Garnish with lemon wedge and serve at once.

Homemade orangeade

pared zest of 2 blood oranges

400 g/1¾ cups white sugar

1 tsp citric acid

550 ml/2⅓ cups freshly squeezed blood orange juice (from about 12 oranges)

chilled soda water or sparkling mineral water, to top up

orange slices, to garnish

SERVES 20

Blood oranges tastes great when made into a syrup for orangeade and they have the most wonderful colour, but don't worry if you can't find these – ordinary oranges will work just as well.

Put the orange zest, sugar, citric acid and 550 ml/2⅓ cups of cold water in a pan and bring to a boil. Simmer, stirring, until all the sugar has dissolved. Add the orange juice and bring the mixture back to the boil, stirring constantly. Remove from the heat and allow to cool for 1 hour. Pour the liquid into a sterilized bottles (see page 4) and it will keep in the fridge for up to 2 months. To serve, pour 50–60 ml/1⅔–2 oz. into ice-filled tumblers, top up with soda water, garnish with an orange slice and serve at once.

Berry smoothie

2 tbsp puréed red berries
  (see page 114)

300 ml/1¼ cups natural/
  plain yogurt

300 ml/1¼ cups milk, chilled

150 g/1 cup fresh strawberries,
  hulled and sliced

250 g/2 cups frozen mixed berries

1 tsp pure vanilla extract

runny honey or agave syrup,
  to taste

fresh strawberries, blackberries
  or raspberries, to garnish
  (optional)

SERVES 2

Replenish your energy levels in the heat with
this berry smoothie full of sumptuous sweetness.
If you'd prefer a dairy-free version of the drink,
use a plant-based yogurt and milk of your choice.

Put the puréed berries in a squeezy bottle and pipe
a spiral onto the inside of each of 2 highball glasses. Put
the yogurt and milk in a blender, add the fresh strawberries,
frozen berries, vanilla extract and honey and blitz until
all the fruit is blended. Pass the smoothie through a
sieve/strainer to remove the seeds, then pour into the
prepared glasses. Thread several berries onto an olive
pick (if using), add to each glass and serve at once.

Blue Hawaii

¼ fresh pineapple, peeled
  and cored

150 ml/⅔ cup coconut water

flesh from ¼ fresh coconut

a generous handful of fresh
  blueberries

1 tsp blue spirulina powder

SERVES 2

This delicious coconut and pineapple smoothie get's
its distinctive colour from fresh blueberries and blue
spirulina powder (see photograph on page 125).

Put the pineapple, coconut water, fresh coconut,
blueberries and spirulina powder in a blender. Blend
together until the coconut flesh is fine and smooth. Pour
the drink into 2 glass tumblers and serve at once.

Glow juice

8 celery sticks
(see Note on page 131)

1 cucumber, peeled

1 eating apple, cored

15 ml/1 tbsp apple cider vinegar

a thumb-sized piece of fresh
ginger, peeled

SERVES 2

Try this unusual super-cooling and refreshing
fruit and vegetable juice and it may well
become your new summer favourite!

Pass all the ingredients through a juicer. Transfer to a
jug/pitcher and place in the fridge. Once chilled, pour
into 2 glass tumblers and serve at once.

Melemele

1 yellow (bell) pepper, deseeded
and quartered

2 yellow carrots, peeled and
roughly chopped

2 yellow apples, such as Golden
Delicious, Opal, Yellow Golden,
etc, cored and roughly chopped

a thumb-sized piece of fresh
ginger, peeled

SERVES 2

This sunshine-filled smoothie makes use of nothing
but yellow ingredients to create a super cleansing
and restorative juice to brighten up your day.

Put all the ingredients into a blender and blitz. Transfer
to a jug/pitcher and place in the fridge. Once chilled,
pour into 2 glass tumblers and serve at once.

Mango passion

100 g/⅔ cup frozen mixed berries, defrosted

1 tbsp icing/confectioners' sugar

1 large fresh mango, peeled and pitted, plus extra slices to garnish

pulp and seeds from 1 passion fruit

chilled soda water or sparkling mineral water, to top up

SERVES 2

An indulgent drink for lovers of the exotic sweetness of mango and passion fruit. Why not enjoy this juice in place of your usual sundowner?

Put the berries in a bowl and add the icing/confectioners' sugar. Mash well with a fork and set aside for 15 minutes, then pass through a fine sieve/strainer. Purée the mango flesh in a blender until smooth and then stir in the passion fruit pulp. Fill 2 highball glasses with ice cubes, divide the berries between the glasses followed by the mango and passion fruit purée. Top up with soda water, garnish each drink with a mango slice and serve at once.

Peach nectar

5 ripe peaches or nectarines, halved, pitted and quartered

freshly squeezed juice of 3 oranges

1 tsp agave syrup or runny honey

SERVES 2

You can use nectarines or peaches here, both of which add a richness to the juice as well as providing a delicious blast off summer fruitiness.

Pass the peaches or nectarines through a juicer. Pour the juice into a jug/pitcher, add the orange juice and agave syrup and stir. Place in the fridge. Once chilled, pour into 2 glass tumblers and serve at once.

Watermelon cooler

1 medium ripe seedless watermelon

freshly squeezed juice of 3 limes

sugar syrup, to taste (see page 8)

lime wedges, to garnish

SERVES 2

Ripe, juicy watermelons are synonymous with summer days and this blended juice is unbeatable!

Using a melon baller, make 6 balls of melon and thread 3 onto each of 2 olive picks. Chill in the fridge until needed. Chop the remaining watermelon flesh, put it in a blender with the lime juice and a few handfuls of ice cubes and blitz until smooth. Taste for sweetness – if it is too sour, add a little sugar syrup and blend again.

Pour into 2 chilled glass tumblers, garnish each drink with a melon-ball stick and a lime wedge and serve at once.

Bondi rip

1 large fresh mango, peeled, pitted and diced

250 ml/1 cup pineapple juice

1 banana, peeled and sliced

50 ml/1⅔ oz. raspberry syrup (see page 9)

SERVES 2

Imagine sipping this mocktail on Australia's most famous beach as the heat of the day fades and the sun worshippers head home for the night...

Put the mango flesh, banana and pineapple juice in a blender. Add a handful of ice cubes and whizz until smooth. Drizzle a little raspberry syrup down the sides of 2 highball glasses, pour in the blended fruit and ice mixture and stir well. Serve at once.

Lime & mint agua fresca

6–8 large fresh mint leaves

3 limes, quartered

130 g/⅔ cup white sugar

SERVES 4

Using the whole lime, skin and all, gives this classic Mexican drink a unique flavour so give it a try!

Put the mint leaves, limes and sugar in a blender with 500 ml/2 cups water and blend for about 2 minutes. Strain the mixture through a sieve/strainer into a large jug/pitcher, add plenty of ice cubes (about 500 g/1 lb 2 oz.) and stir well. Top up the jug/pitcher with cold water until it reaches 2 litres/quarts and stir well again.

Variation: If you'd like your drink with some bubbles, substitute still for sparkling water at the topping-up stage.

Green juice with cactus

1 celery stick, plus a leaf to garnish (see Note)

1 nopal leaf (an edible leaf from a prickly pear cactus – available to buy online from specialist retailers)

freshly squeezed juice of 1 orange

a flat-leaf parsley sprig

SERVES 1

This Mexican juice blend is well worth a try, and not just for the health benefits of the cactus!

Cut the celery into 4 pieces and slice the nopal leaf into 4–6 strips. Put both in a blender with the orange juice, parsley and 200 ml/generous ¾ cup water. Blend for about 2 minutes, until smooth. Pour into a highball glass, garnish with a celery leaf and serve at once.

Note: It is worth trying to get rid of as many of the sinewy threads of the celery as you can. Do this by gently snapping off the end and then pulling away the threads that hang on to it. The general rule is the fresher the celery, the fewer the threads.

English summer punch

Apples and cherries are a great flavour pairing and have been combined
in desserts with great results over the years. The good news is, they
work just as well in this delicious alcohol-free summer punch.

125 g/1 cup fresh sweet cherries,
pitted

400 g/2 cups white sugar

1.5 litres/6 cups cloudy apple juice

freshly squeezed juice of 4 limes

200 ml/generous ¾ cup chilled
soda or sparkling mineral water,
to top up

10 fresh cherries, to garnish

SERVES 10

Put the cherries in a blender and blitz for 1 minute. Put
the blended cherries, sugar and 1 cup/250 ml water in
a saucepan set over low heat. Heat gently, stirring
frequently, until the sugar is dissolved. Remove from the
heat and leave to cool.

Combine the cooled cherry syrup, apple juice and lime
juice in a large jug/pitcher filled with ice cubes and stir
gently to mix. Pour into highball or hurricane glasses filled
with crushed ice and top up with soda water. Garnish each
drink with a cherry and serve at once.

Triple goddess

150 ml/5 oz. pomegranate juice

150 ml/5 oz. cloudy apple juice

freshly squeezed juice of 1½ limes

25 ml/¾ oz. elderflower cordial

soda or sparkling mineral water,
  to top up

apple fans, to garnish

SERVES 2

Pomegranate, apple, elderflower and lime combine to create a tangy effervescence in this elegant mocktail. Try to find a pomegranate juice that errs on the slightly bitter side and the drink will balance perfectly, offset by the sweetness of the apple juice and sugary cordial.

Combine the fruit juices and elderflower cordial in a jug/pitcher. Stir gently to mix and divide between 2 ice-filled highball glasses. Top up each drink with soda, garnish with an apple fan and serve at once.

Raspberry & apple fizz

300 g/2¼ cups frozen raspberries

250 ml/1 cup cloudy apple juice

soda or sparkling mineral water,
  to top up

fresh raspberries and apple slices,
  to garnish (optional)

SERVES 2

This is a truly refreshing juice for a hot summer's day, and with the addition of the soda or sparkling water it makes a delightful mocktail that can be prepared in seconds.

Put the raspberries, apple juice and 12 ice cubes in a blender and blitz until smooth. Pour into 2 highball glasses and top up with soda water. Garnish each drink with a few raspberries and an apple slice (if using) and serve at once.

Strawberry lemonade

20 ripe fresh strawberries

finely grated zest and freshly squeezed juice of 4 lemons

6 tbsp white sugar

a large handful of fresh mint leaves

soda or sparkling mineral water, to top up

lemon slices, to garnish

SERVES 2

Homemade lemonade combined with blended strawberries and fresh mint is as pleasing a drink on a hot summer's day as you can imagine!

Put the strawberries in a blender and blitz to a purée. Add the lemon zest and juice, sugar and mint to a large jug/pitcher and stir until the sugar has dissolved. Fill the pitcher with ice cubes, add the blended strawberries and top up with soda water.

Pour into 2 ice-filled highball glasses, garnish each drink with a lemon slice and serve at once.

Lemon & ginger barley water

125 g/²/₃ cup pearl barley

finely grated zest and juice of 4 lemons

100 g/½ cup brown sugar

5-cm/2-in. piece of fresh ginger, peeled and roughly grated

lemon slices, to garnish

SERVES 4–6

Lemon barley water is an old-fashioned health drink that is surprisingly easy to make at home.

Wash the barley and place in a large bowl with the lemon zest, sugar and ginger. Pour 1.2 litres/5 cups boiling water over the mixture and allow to cool for several hours. When the mixture is cold, add the lemon juice and strain into a jug/pitcher and transfer to the fridge. Once chilled divide between ice-filled glass tumblers, garnish each drink with a lemon slice and serve at once.

Summer garden

4-cm/1½-in. piece of cucumber,
  plus extra to garnish

5 fresh basil leaves

1 tsp sugar syrup (see page 8)

1 tsp freshly squeezed lemon juice

chilled sparkling elderflower drink,
  to top up

SERVES 1

This is lovely drink, perfect for summer garden parties. Simply scale up the base mix ingredients, add a little to each glass and top up with the fizz.

Cut the cucumber into small chunks and place in a cocktail shaker with the basil and sugar syrup. Muddle well to release all the juice. Add a handful of ice cubes, stir well and then strain into a chilled Champagne flute. Top up with sparkling elderflower drink, garnish with a long strip of cucumber and serve at once.

Strawberry fields forever

2 fresh strawberries,
  plus extra to garnish

15 ml/½ oz. strawberry syrup
  (see page 8)

a few fresh mint leaves (optional)

1 tsp freshly squeezed lemon juice

chilled alcohol-free sparkling wine,
  to top up

SERVES 1

This is guaranteed hit on a balmy summer evening wherever you are. You can find very good alcohol-free sparkling wines, choose a dry one to use here.

Halve the strawberries and place them in a cocktail shaker with the strawberry syrup and the mint (if using). Muddle to release the juices. Add the lemon juice and a handful of ice cubes and shake well. Strain into a chilled Champagne flute and top with alcohol-free sparkling wine. Garnish with a strawberry slice and serve at once.

Tropical spice smoothie

½ large pineapple, peeled, cored and chopped

1 banana, peeled and chopped

200 ml/generous ¾ cup natural/plain yogurt

100 ml/⅓ cup coconut milk

½ tsp ground ginger

1 tsp runny honey or agave syrup

1 tsp freshly squeezed lime juice

seeds from 3 cardamom pods, ground

finely grated lime zest, to garnish

SERVES 2

Rich and nurturing, this smoothie is a delicious combination of tropical fruit and spices. When choosing a pineapple, tug one of the leaves on top and if it comes away easily, it is ready to eat.

Put the pineapple, banana, yogurt, coconut milk, ginger, honey and lime juice in blender and blend until smooth and creamy. Stir in the ground cardamom. Divide between 2 chilled glass tumblers, sprinkle with a little lime zest and serve at once.

Berry bright smoothie

2 handfuls of fresh blueberries

2 handfuls of frozen or fresh raspberries

freshly squeezed juice of 2 large oranges

2 tsp runny honey or agave syrup

2 tbsp jumbo oats

2 tsp açaí berry powder

SERVES 2

This delicious berry-rich smoothie has the addition of oats which make it rich and creamy and suitable as a summer breakfast in a glass to enjoy whilst sitting in the garden.

Put the blueberries, raspberries, orange juice, honey, oats and açaí berry powder in a blender and blend until smooth. Divide between 2 chilled glass tumblers and serve at once.

Index

Recipe credits

BEN REED
Anejo highball
Bay breeze
Berry caipiroska
Berry Collins
Bourbon cobbler
Classic sangria
English summer punch
Hedgerow sling
Hibiscus martini
Hurricane
Italian sour
Jalisco siesta
Moscow mule
Pineapple pisco punch
Planter's punch
Pomegranate punch
Raspberry rickey
Rose-tinted spectacles
Shirley Temple
Singapore sling
Strawberry lemonade
Triple goddess
Watermelon martini
White sangria

LAURA GLADWIN
Airmail
Bellini rum punch
Cocomango
El rosso
Florida breeze

Hugo
Nonna's garden
Peach julep
Pimm's deluxe
Prosecco iced tea
Prosecco passion
Sbagliato
Seventh heaven
Sgroppino
Sparkling mojito
St Clement's fizz
Strawberry fields forever
Summer garden
The perfect spritz
Tiziano

JESSES ESTES
Ancho margarita
Batanga 2
Bourbon spritz
Derby julep
El diablo
Georgia mint julep
Hibiscus highball
Honi honi
Lion's tail
Marquee
Matador
Mint julep
Paloma
Pomegranate margarita
Primavera punch

JULIA CHARLES
Cherry vanilla kiss
Classic strawberry frosé

Just peachy punch
Rosé spritz
Sgroppinko
Spanish fruit cup
Sparkling Mediterranean
 punch
Spicy ginger & berry cooler
Strawberry spritz
Tutti frutti
Twisted pineapple frosé
Watermelon, lime & mint
 frosé
West Coast sunset

HANNAH MILES
Berry smoothie
Blueberry bubble slushie
Firecracker popsicle slushie
Mint julep slushie
Pina colada slushie
Raspberry ripple float
Sea breeze slushie
Watermelon cooler

JAMES PORTER
Blue Hawaii
Glow juice
Hibiscus G&T
Island daisy
Mango daiquiri

LOUISE PICKFORD
Bondi rip
Mango passion
Orange sunset
Raspberry & apple fizz

Raspberry, lychee
 & apple juice
Sea breeze

**BEN FORDHAM & FELIPE
FUENTES CRUZ**
Green juice with cactus
Lime & mint agua fresca
Spicy green margarita
Tommy's margarita

VALERIE AIKMAN-SMITH
Cucumber martini
Pisco sour
Spiced almond horchata
 float

NICOLA GRAIMES
Berry bright smoothie
Peach & orange nectar
Tropical spice smoothie

DAVID T. SMITH
Gimlet gin tonica
Gin tonica float

URSULA FERRIGNO
Lemon & ginger barley
 water
Tropical mojito

VICTORIA GLASS
Dark & stormy float

BESHLIE GRIMES
Homemade orangeade

Photography credits

All photography by
ALEX LUCK, with the
following exceptions:

PETER CASSIDY
Pages 26 and 131

GARETH MORGANS
Pages 22, 25, 46, 50, 53,
91, 119, 120 & 127

WILLIAM LINGWOOD
Pages 5 (top centre) 65, 66,
95, 97, 101, 110, 117, 132
& 135

MOWIE KAY
Front and back endpapers;
Page 123

ERIN KUNKEL
Page 29

STEVE PAINTER
Pages 1 & 3

TOBY SCOTT
Page 69

KATE WHITAKER
Pages 92, 123 & 140

CLARE WINFIELD
Front cover; Pages 11 & 35